A Newbies Guide to Kindle

Minute Help Press

SOME PEOPLE ONLY HAVE A FEW MINUTES TO SPARE

Minute Help Guides

Minute Help Press

www.minutehelp.com

Table of Contents

INTRODUCTION 3

PART 1: THE BASICS 4

WHAT'S IN THE BOX (AND WHAT'S NOT) 5

POWERING UP, GETTING ONLINE 6

NAVIGATION, GETTING AROUND 8

AMAZON STORES AND CONTENT 10

THE CAROUSEL 13

PART 2: GETTING MORE OUT OF YOUR KINDLE FIRE HD 15

AMAZON PRIME 16

X-RAY FOR MOVIES AND TV SHOWS 18

X-RAY FOR BOOKS 19

IMMERSION READING 21

LENDING, GIFTING AND FREE BOOK RESOURCES 24

Lending *24*

Gifting *25*

Free Book Resources *26*

Adding Your Book, Music and Movie Collections *27*

WEB BROWSING 31

EMAIL, CONTACTS, CALENDAR 33

SKYPE, FACEBOOK AND TWITTER 34

PART 3: ADVANCED TIPS AND TRICKS (AND MUST-HAVE APPS) 37

SETTINGS 38

SIDELOADING APPS 41

APPENDIX: THE BEST DOWNLOADS FOR YOUR NEW KINDLE 42

GAMES APPS 42

APPS 44

ABOUT MINUTE HELP PRESS 46

Introduction

Amazon has raised the bar with their new line of Kindle HD tablets. Not content to rest on their reputation as the world's leading purveyor of eBooks, Amazon is giving Apple a run for its money with this series of low-cost, high-performance machines. Whichever model you've chosen, you've just bought yourself an incredibly powerful handheld entertainment device that *should* cost a lot more than it does: the company is banking on the fact that you'll be using your Kindle Fire HD to find and purchase all kinds of things from Amazon.com.

If this is your first tablet experience, it can all feel a little overwhelming: the App Store, X-Ray, Kindle Prime, all of this stuff can sound like science fiction to the uninitiated. Amazon has done their best to make it as easy as possible, heavily customizing the open-source Android operating system for both ease-of-use and reliability. You might get a little confused at first, but with the help of this guide, we'll have you up and running like a pro within minutes.

Let's get started!

Part 1: The Basics

What's in the Box (and What's Not)

When your brand-new Kindle Fire HD arrives at your door, the first thing you'll notice is the packaging: the black, gingerbread house-style box coupled with the embossed, simple black lettering is certainly eye-catching: in fact, it practically screams, *"super-advanced technology inside!"*

Inside that box, you'll find pretty much everything you need to get started:

- The Kindle Fire HD Device
- A USB Charging Cable
- A "Quick Start Guide"

For some reason, Amazon neglected to include a wall charger accessory with the device. This is an important detail: if you don't have one hanging around, you're probably going to want to pick one up: it can take over 13 hours to charge the device via a traditional USB port on your computer. A wall charger cuts that down to about 4 hours. Any wall charger with a USB port connection will do, so before you spend the money, look around your house for one. Compatible chargers can include those made for:

- Cell Phones
- iPads and Other Tablet Devices
- Any Other Kindle
- Other eReader Devices (Nook, Kobo, Sony Reader, etc.)

If you've got one, great! If not, we suggest heading to your local electronics store: Best Buy, Target or Wal-Mart will almost certainly have what you need. For the absolute cheapest solution, eBay has dozens of different options, some for as little as a dollar or two. Shipping, however, might take a little longer than you'd like. Amazon definitely also carries them, but the price might be a little higher.

*Of course, you may opt to not purchase a wall charger at all, especially if you're only a moderate user. We only mention it because we know how hard it is to wait for any device to charge. Amazon recently announced that they'll knock $10 off the price of their PowerFast wall charger for people who've purchased the Kindle Fire HD. We're not sure how long the deal will last, but check Amazon.com for details.

The included Quick-Start Guide is nothing more than a small piece of paper that tells you where all the buttons are, and what they do. It's actually somewhat easy to forget; they're pretty recessed, and the device is meant to work in every position you can hold it in. For our purposes, we'll call the area that houses the headphone jack, volume buttons, and on/off switch the top.

Powering Up, Getting Online

Once you've located the power button, give it a quick press to turn the device on. Be patient, as the first time can seem like it's taking *forever*. Don't worry; it'll be much quicker next time.

> *In case you didn't already know, this process is called "booting up", just like with your personal computer.*

A lot of complicated stuff is happening in the background, but all you'll see is the Kindle Fire logo. It shouldn't take any longer than a couple of minutes. Once you're past the Kindle Fire screen, you'll be presented with this:

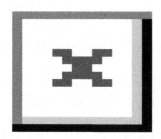

Go ahead and click on your WiFi network. If you've got your home network password protected, a window and a keyboard will pop up: enter your WiFi password here. If you don't know it, consult the person who set up the network. There's an option to skip this part of the setup, but there isn't a whole lot you can do with the device without connecting to the Internet. Once that's finished, the next screen will allow you to register your Kindle. This is another important step, allowing your device to sync with your Amazon account (more on this later).

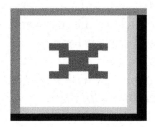

Enter the email address and password that you use on Amazon.com. It'll take a moment to register. If you don't have an Amazon.com account, click the button that says "Create Account" and follow the steps. It only takes a couple of minutes, but make sure you have a credit card handy: it wil store it for you, allowing you to take advantage of Amazon's famous "one-click-purchase" system.

The next screen will ask you to confirm the name on your account. If everything's good, click continue. If not, you might've entered someone else's email. Perhaps you share an Amazon account with someone, which is perfectly fine.

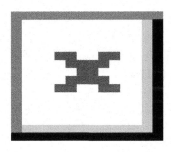

If the name bothers you, you may want to consider getting your own Amazon account, as the user name will appear prominently on the device, pretty much all the time.

Next, you'll be presented with the opportunity to add your social networks. This is actually a really neat thing. Amazon has integrated Facebook and Twitter pretty well into the Kindle Fire HD, allowing you to easily share cool stuff: everything from passages of books you're reading to apps you're using. If you're interested, just click on the icons and a keyboard will pop up. Input your information and the Kindle Fire HD will store it for you.

> *A lot of people have privacy concerns with Facebook and Twitter integration. Amazon has promised to treat your personal info with the respect it deserves, but as always, if you're uncomfortable, opt out.*

That's it. Now we're on the homescreen and ready to explore.

Navigation, Getting Around

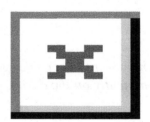

Now we're on the home screen. It looks kind of empty, doesn't it? Don't worry; we're going to fill it up with all kinds of content soon. But first, let's take a look at the layout, and learn how to navigate our way around.

First things first: gestures. The Kindle Fire HD has a very responsive touch screen, requiring just a few different movements out of you to get anywhere you want to go. To wake the device, press the power button briefly, then swipe right to left on the orange swipe bar. After that, it's mostly a simple matter of swiping left or right on the screen to move left and right, and swiping up and down to navigate up and down. Tap with your finger to select an item, or to open an app, a book, a movie, or whatever other content you have. If you tap within a text field, the keyboard will automatically pop up, allowing you to type whatever information you need to.

Along the top of the device, you'll notice several things: first, your name should appear in the left-hand corner. If you have any notifications (an app that requires updating, a new email message, etc) then a number will appear just to the right of that. Moving to the right, we have a clock, and then images representing any active connections (Bluetooth or Wi-Fi). All the way to the right is the battery icon.

Swiping from the top down will bring up what's called the Notification Menu. It includes (obviously) your notifications, but also a few common menu items. Clicking on any of these items will allow you to adjust some common settings like brightness, volume, Wi-Fi, Bluetooth, and orientation. Clicking on any notification will take you to whatever application the notification is referring to:

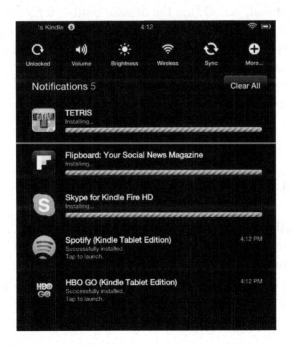

Next, we have the search bar. Computer users will no doubt be familiar with this, and it functions in pretty much the same way, with one exception: you can search three distinct areas for what you want: your personal library of content, Amazon's various web stores, and the Web. Just tap your finger and the keyboard will automatically come up.

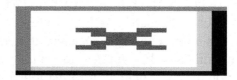

Along the bottom of the device, you'll notice a black bar with a bunch of icons. This area is important for navigating within menus and apps. It won't always look exactly like it does in the illustration above, but it will always serve the same purpose:

On the left is the *Home* icon. This will take you from wherever you are back to the home screen. It comes in handy for leaving applications. To the right of that is the arrow-shaped *Back* button. That will take you back to the previous screen. In the middle, you'll find a *Context* menu button. This can include a number of different, helpful functions, and what's shown there will depend on what you're doing. To the right of that, you'll find the *Search* button, a handy shortcut to the search bar we just discussed. The little star in the corner, otherwise known as the *Favorite* button, allows you to favorite any item. The favorites menu is accessible from the home screen, and it comes in handy as a place to put your most-used applications.

Now that you've got the basics down, let's add some content.

Amazon Stores and Content

Amazon has made it incredibly easy to purchase content on the Kindle Fire HD, and rightly so: that's where they make their money. Thankfully, they also organize all that content pretty well for you. Just below the search bar on the home screen, you'll see a left-to-right menu. These different items will take you wherever you want to go. Let's take a quick look at each one.

Shop - This will take you to every store that Amazon operates. Stores are separated into a few different broad categories: books, apps, movies and videos, and physical goods. You can reach any of them from here, and you're only one click away from downloading and using whatever you want.

Games – This serves as a repository for all the games you've purchased. Amazon will store all of your purchases for later download, so you don't have to clog up your system with games you've already played. On the right side of the menu, you'll see a link to the Amazon App Store labeled "store."

Apps – This one is a little strange. It's (presumably) meant to hold all of your non-game applications (Skype, Facebook, IMDB, etc.) but it actually holds everything, games included. Again, you'll find a link to the App Store on the right.

> *While some people complain that Amazon's App Store isn't as large as the Google Play Store that it's based on, the Amazon App Store allows you to download one chosen app for free every single day. It's usually a game, but you can't do any better than free, right?*

Books - This area is reserved for, you guessed it, books. Any Kindle Books you've ever purchased are waiting here, ready for you to read them. It takes a little bit of effort to make the Kindle Fire HD recognize books you may have downloaded from elsewhere, but we'll get into that a little later. Tapping the Store link this time will send you right to the Kindle Store, where you can find hundreds of thousands of books to read, a good bit of them either free or very competitively priced. Tapping any book in your library will open it for reading.

> *Tapping or swiping on the left or right moves you forward or backward within the book, but tapping and holding on a word will bring up the highlight menu. Once the highlight menu is activated (you'll see it begin to highlight, it's bright purple) you can drag your finger to select as much of the text as you like. It comes in very handy for sharing passages with friends via Facebook and other apps, which we'll explore a little later.*

Music – This area holds your Amazon music collection. Anything previously purchased will show up here, and, of course, there is a handy link to the Amazon Music Store, where you can purchase some more. Just like with apps, Amazon will keep your music in the cloud until you're ready to listen to it, saving your Kindle Fire HD some space.

> *Amazon actually has a pretty neat solution for your music collection, which we'll discuss at length a little later in the book.*

Videos – This space is dedicated to all of your favorite movies and TV shows. Strictly for Amazon and personally owned content, apps like Netflix and HBO GO don't show up here. The Store is particularly useful if you're an Amazon Prime subscriber, which we'll get into a little bit later.

Newsstand – Just like Apple, Amazon is heavily promoting digital magazine subscriptions. Digital magazines look great on the Kindle Fire HD, given its high-resolution screen. The magazines are generally not just a copy of the magazines you can find in the store; they contain interactive content and extras exclusive to the digital domain. The *Newsstand* menu holds all of your magazine subscriptions, and gives you access to the Magazine Store, where many of the magazines Amazon offers are available on a free-to-try basis.

Audiobooks - This section is basically a portal to the Audible.com collection of audiobooks. Amazon is doing some pretty interesting things with so-called "immersion reading", which we'll discuss a little later, but you might find the (relatively) high cost of standalone audiobooks might outweigh the convenience.

Web – This is a shortcut to Amazon's web browser. Dubbed Silk, it's claimed to offer browsing speeds up to 40% faster than competing tablets. We're a little dubious of that claim, but the Kindle Fire HD is definitely a convenient way to browse the Internet.

Photos – The Kindle Fire HD, unlike its predecessor, comes equipped with a camera. While it's not the most powerful camera in the world, it still takes some pretty decent pictures under the right circumstances. Your device's photos will appear here for you to look through, edit, share, or delete.

> *Unlike the original Kindle, the Kindle Fire HD has a very easy way to capture whatever appears on your screen. To take a "screen shot", simply press the power button and the volume down button at the exact same time. It might take a little practice to get the timing right, but you'll know you've succeeded when you see the screen briefly flash.*

Docs – Loading your personal documents to the Kindle Fire HD is a fairly straightforward process. You can email documents to your Kindle email address, which is usually the beginning of the email address you used when setting up the device, with @kindle.com appended to it. Once you've done that, your documents will appear here. It's useful for reading your computer's Word documents on the go.

Offers - A controversial move on Amazon's part, there's a chance that this section may not even exist by the time you read this. Basically, in order to save you a couple bucks on the price of your Kindle Fire HD, they've turned the lock screen of the device into an ever-changing digital billboard, advertising everything from books to airline tickets. This section contains the ads you've already seen, just in case you're interested in anything they have to offer.

> *Amazon recently announced that they'll turn off the built-in "offers" for a $15 fee. Even though it's tantamount to extortion, we recommend doing it: those ads can be pretty distracting.*

The Carousel

Once you've added some content from the above sources, they will show up in their rightful menu places, but they'll also show up in that blank space in the middle. This is called the Carousel. It houses all of your most recently used apps and content, giving you quick access to whatever you're doing. While your content will obviously not be the same, your Carousel will look something like this after awhile:

To remove an item from your Carousel, simply tap and hold: it'll bring up a menu. You can also delete items from the device from here. This is convenient, as sometimes things you don't necessarily need show up here; web pages, books you've already finished, or screen shots you've already emailed. There is also a shortcut to add items to your favorites for quicker access:

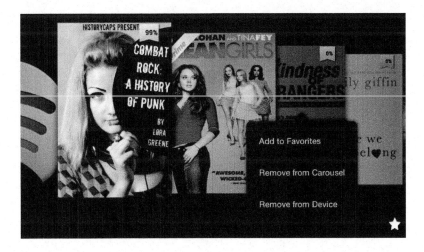

Part 2: Getting More Out of Your Kindle Fire HD

Amazon Prime

If you've never used it before, your Kindle Fire HD comes with a special surprise: a free month of something called Amazon Prime. What's that, you ask? Well, it's a few things:

- A Netflix-like unlimited television and movie streaming service
- A lending library
- Free two-day shipping on just about anything Amazon sells

The cost for the service is $79 a year, which is actually significantly cheaper than Netflix's $120, though with Amazon, you'll have to pay the whole amount upfront. Their streaming catalog isn't *quite* as expansive as Netflix, though if you're a Netflix user, you already know that at least 50% of their offerings consist of absolute garbage like "Crocosaurus vs. Mega Albino Gorilla." Amazon Prime focuses on quality, not quantity.

The lending library is another great feature: it allows you to borrow a book a month from a library of thousands of Kindle titles. While there are some definite awful titles in the mix (*50 Shades of Obama?!*), the superstars also make an appearance: as of this writing, The Harry Potter books and the Hunger Games Trilogy are both available to borrow free of charge. You only get one book a month, though, so choose wisely.

The free shipping may or may not apply to you, but it's a definite money saver. Amazon sells everything from books and movies to televisions and almonds, often at bargain-basement prices. You're pretty much guaranteed to save a little money, especially if you live in a state where Amazon isn't required to collect sales tax.

While Amazon has said that the activation of your Amazon Prime trial should be automatic, in our case it wasn't. We had to sign up at **www.amazon.com/prime** to take advantage of the trial. Also, since we had to sign up on the web site, we were automatically enrolled in the "auto draft" of the $79 yearly price. If we hadn't noticed in time, we would've been stuck for the money (whether we wanted to continue the service or not). Just in case, here's how to avoid that:

Immediately after signing up for the free Amazon Prime trial on your computer, head the Amazon's homepage, **www.amazon.com**. Over on the right, you'll see a menu labeled Your Account:

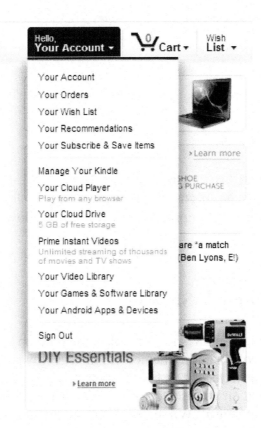

Hover over it and click the first item, it will be labeled Your Account. From there, you'll see a whole host of options. Scroll down to the Settings area and look for the words "Manage Prime Membership." Click on it.

Settings
Password, Prime & E-mail

Account Settings

Change Account Settings
Name, e-mail, password and mobile
phone

Forgot Your Password?

1-Click Settings

Manage Prime Membership

Amazon Student Membership

Amazon Mom Membership

Manage Text Tracking Alerts

Amazon Tax Exemption Program

The next screen will be full of details about your Prime membership, but all you need to concern yourself with is the top left corner, which will look like this:

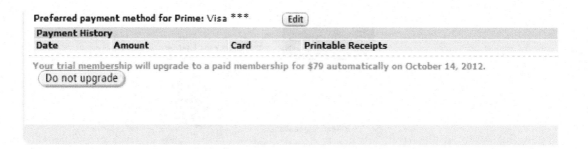

Just click that "Do Not Upgrade" button and confirm. That's it. You can still enjoy your Amazon Prime trial until the 30 days are up. If you decide to fork over the dough for the annual subscription, just head back to **www.amazon.com/prime** and follow the prompts.

X-Ray For Movies and TV Shows

Have you ever paused a movie or a TV show to look something up? It's frustrating to stop what you're doing to figure out who what's-her-name with the eyebrows is, and what other movie you know her from. Amazon aims to rectify that with a new service called X-Ray. Simply put, Amazon puts all that info right on your screen, a tap away, so that you don't have to stop what you're doing to ask a friend or consult Wikipedia. It utilizes the excellent IMDB database, too, so you know the information is both accurate and up to date.

To use it, simply start watching a movie. Tap anywhere on the screen and the X-Ray icon will show up on the left-hand side of the screen. Click on it, and you can view all sorts of information about the cast of the movie. In this example, we queued up "Mean Girls" on Amazon Prime:

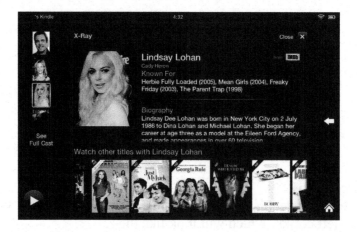

As you can see, we clicked on the star of the movie, Lindsay Lohan, and were brought to a page within the movie screen. We can see her biography, her notable roles, and other Lindsay Lohan movies that are available for instant streaming. The coolest part? X-Ray will show you the same information for everyone in the movie, and it'll be front and center during the time they're on the screen. For instance, early in "Mean Girls" there is a very brief scene involving some home-schooled children. Bringing up X-Ray at this point will highlight those children:

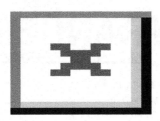

*Due to copyright restrictions, we're unable to show you any screenshots with footage from "Mean Girls" included, but you get the idea.

X-Ray for Books

Not content to let their X-Ray technology be exclusive to the moving image, Amazon has also added it to books. While not every book is optimized for X-Ray, the ones that are display some very neat (and sometimes useful) information. We borrowed a book from Amazon Prime called "The Kindness of Strangers" to show you how it works.

"The Kindness of Strangers" follows a man on a journey around America. He is homeless and penniless and has to rely on, you guessed it, the *kindness of strangers* to survive. He has better luck in some places than in others. If you want to find out his thoughts on, say, the great state of Montana, you'd normally have to thumb through it yourself, or use a cumbersome search function. Now, you just have to hit the X-Ray button:

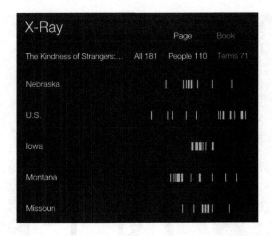

The same technology also works for character names and themes. It's a great way to navigate a book.

Immersion Reading

Another interesting technology that Amazon is debuting with the Kindle Fire HD is called Immersion Reading. Simply put, immersion reading allows you to listen to narration of your downloaded books while reading along. Not just the standard robot voice speech-to-text thing, Amazon has partnered with Audible.com to bring you professional audiobook narration, often at significantly discounted prices. It's also built right in to the purchase of compatible eBooks, with a handy one-click option. There are somewhere around 15,000 Immersion-capable books in the store as of this writing, and even a smattering of free ones.

To get started, just open up the Amazon Book Store and scroll towards the bottom of the main page. There you should see a selection of Immersion Reading titles. Click "see all" and it will bring up a category view of your options:

You'll notice that there are a few free titles listed prominently at the top. We downloaded "A Tale of Two Cities" to show you how it works.

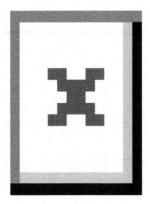

After we've downloaded the book, right next to the green "Read Now" button, an "Add Immersion Reading" button appears. Simply tap it, and it'll begin downloading. The files seem to take a couple of minutes to download, so be patient. Go ahead and open the book you downloaded. Tap in the middle of the page to bring up the menu, you should see this on the bottom:

Simply press play to begin the Immersion Reading experience. The software will automatically highlight the text as the narrator reads it.

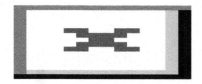

To stop the Immersion Reading experience at any time, simple tap the middle of the page again to bring up the menu. Press the play button again to stop the narration.

A great thing about the Immersion Reading technology is that Amazon has added it to its Whispersync system: your place will automatically be saved from device-to-device.

Lending, Gifting and Free Book Resources

After spending a few minutes with your new Kindle Fire HD, it's pretty easy to see how quickly you can empty your bank account with constant content purchases. There are ways to minimize the expense, a few of them even officially endorsed by Amazon.

Lending

Most eBooks downloaded from the Kindle store can be lent, library-style, to anyone you like. It's pretty simple to do, and a much better way to let people borrow books, because you know where they are and can take them back whenever you want. It's not as seamless a process as it could be, but you can do it straight from your Kindle Fire HD in just a few steps.

First, head over to the Kindle Store. Once there, you should see a context menu in the middle of the bottom navigation bar. Tap it to bring up the menu:

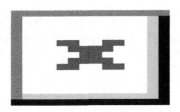

Tap the menu item called "Manage Your Kindle." This will bring up the Amazon.com page associated with your account. You may have to verify your login details here. Once you're in, you'll see a list of your Kindle books, and little "action" menus to the right of each title. Tap the "action" menu to bring up the options:

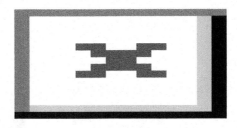

Tap "Loan This Title" and you'll be brought to the lending page. Simply fill it out, making sure to type the name of the recipient's email address properly. Tap "Send Now" and you're done.

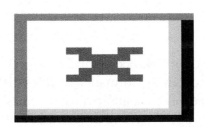

Gifting

Giving eBooks on the Kindle Fire HD is also a sort-of convoluted process. After finding the title you'd like to give as a gift, simply scroll all the way down the description until you see the phrase "View This Title on Amazon.com." Tap it.

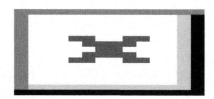

You've now brought up your chosen book's Amazon page. Notice on the right that you have several purchasing options. To give the book as a gift, simply click "Give as Gift" and fill out the form. That's it.

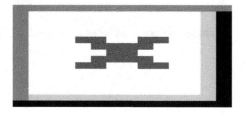

Free Book Resources

There are thousands upon thousands of free books available on the Internet. Chances are, your local library even has a collection of Kindle formatted eBooks that you can borrow just like their physical counterparts. There are, however, some specific free book resources that you'll want to learn about and take advantage of. You'll have to download these books to your computer and transfer them to the Kindle Fire HD manually, but we'll walk you through that in the next section.

Project Gutenberg (**www.gutenberg.org**) is the oldest and most well-known online book repository, and for good reason: they've been at it since 1971. Seriously. At present, they have over 40,000 completely free eBooks to offer, a lot of them classics. This is your first stop if you want to build up a gigantic collection, or teach your kids about classic literature.

The Internet Archive (**www.archive.org**) is another great resource, and not just for books. They've been archiving the entire internet for twenty years. For such a little known resource, their contribution to the world has been enormous. They've got over a million different texts to offer, but it'll take you awhile to comb through it for the gems.

> *Archive.org also has an extensive collection of live recordings from all kinds of bands: everyone from The Grateful Dead to 311 to Hank Williams III can be found and downloaded to your Kindle Fire HD.*

The Open Library (**www.openlibrary.org**) is probably the easiest to navigate of all. Their ambitious plan is to become the Wikipedia of books, and with over 200,000 free to download eBooks, they're well on their way. Many library systems use The Open Library as their online lending service for patrons and It's easy to see why: the layout is simple, yet concise, allowing you to find something great with just a few clicks.

Librovox (**www.librovox.org**) is easily the best resource for free audiobooks. They've got thousands of them, mostly classics, available to download in either MP3 or OGG format. Copying these files to your Kindle Fire HD takes a little bit of work, but the quality you get (not to mention the price!) makes it absolutely worth it if audiobooks are your thing.

Adding Your Book, Music and Movie Collections

Given that Amazon makes the majority of their money by selling you content for your Kindle Fire HD, it makes sense that they wouldn't exactly make it easy for you to add the content you've already purchased somewhere else to the device. Thankfully, it's a pretty straightforward process once you've done it once.

> *These instructions are intended for Windows users, but the process should be nearly identical for all you Apple enthusiasts.*

Music - There are two ways of getting your music files to the Kindle Fire HD. First, we'll use Amazon's method. It's called Cloud Player. Cloud Player will allow you to upload up to 250 songs for free. Amazon will store them in your account, and then send a high-quality 256kb/s copy to your device whenever you want. It's a handy, no-nonsense solution for anyone who doesn't really have a whole lot of music.

Amazon supports MP3, of course, but also Apple's preferred format, AAC (.M4A), provided your iTunes files are pretty new. Apple used to use an invasive digital rights management (DRM) solution, but they cut that out a few years ago. DRM-enabled files won't work on the Kindle Fire.

On your computer, point your web browser to **www.cloudplayer.com**. Agree to the terms of service, and log in using your Amazon account details if prompted. From there, you'll be presented with this:

Click on the button that says "Import Your Music." This will prompt you to install a program called Amazon Music Importer.

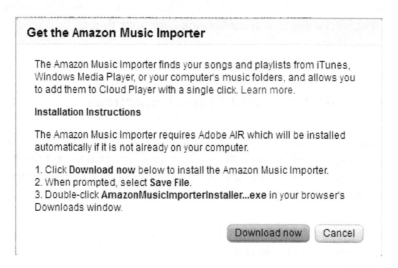

Install the program as you would any other. After that's finished, it will automatically launch. You'll be given two options: start scan or browse manually. If you choose to start scan, the program will search your entire computer for files to upload. Browsing manually allows you to choose specific files to upload. For this example, we manually uploaded an album that we ripped ourselves from CD, "El Camino" by The Black Keys.

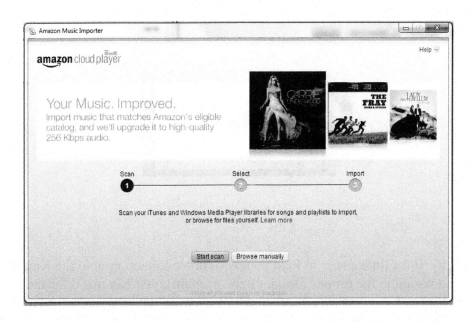

After clicking Browse manually, we pointed the program to the folder and hit ok. The rest of the work was done for us, taking about 2 minutes. As soon as that's done, the album instantly appeared on the Kindle Fire HD, ready for playing.

The second method is a little easier. First, connect your Kindle Fire HD to any available USB port on your computer. Windows should automatically detect it after a few moments. Once it has, open an explorer menu. You should see this:

Click on Kindle and then double click on Internal Storage. From there, find the folder labeled music and double click that. From there, drag and drop the music you'd like to copy into this folder. We're using "Four" by Bloc Party, another album that we ripped ourselves from CD. Windows may warn you that the files might not be playable and ask you whether or not you'd like to continue. Ignore that. Once the files have finished copying, the album will instantly appear on the Kindle Fire HD, alongside the album we just finished uploading to Cloud Player:

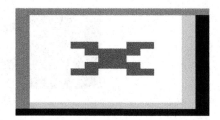

Books- Thankfully, it's a little easier to load your own book collection onto the Kindle Fire HD. Provided your books are in the proper format (.azw or .mobi), you can just drag and drop your books into the "books" folder on your Kindle, just like we did with the album above. If your eBooks are in a different format (ePub, HTML, etc) then we have to put a little more effort in.

First, head to **www.calibre-ebook.com** and download the free Calibre eBook management software. Installation is easy, just follow the prompts. When it's finished installing, open the program and you'll be greeted with this:

Over on the top left, you'll see an icon marked "add books." Clicking it will open the add books menu. Select "add books from a single directory" and point the file browser to whatever book you'd like to add.

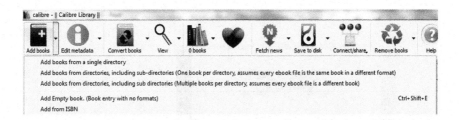

For this example, we're going to use a book that we downloaded from iTunes called "Hemingway's Boat." The book is in Apple's preferred format, ePub, so we need to convert it to an Amazon compatible format before sending it to the Kindle Fire HD. Once your book has been imported, just click the convert book button on the top. Set the output to .mobi and wait for it to convert.

Once that's done, right click on the file and click on "show in folder." Then, simply drag the newly created mobi version of your book into the books folder of your Kindle Fire HD. That's it.

Movies – Just like eBooks and music files, Amazon won't allow you to copy just *any* movie format to your Kindle Fire HD. You're pretty much limited to .MP4. If your movie files are in this format, great: Just drag and drop them into the movies folder on your Kindle Fire HD. If not, you'll have to convert them, which is a far more tedious and difficult process than with eBooks. We recommend looking into Handbrake, a Windows/Mac conversion tool. It's available free of charge from **www.handbrake.fr**, though we have to warn you, it's not for the inexperienced. In fact, a tutorial on Handbrake is beyond the scope of this guide, though their website has some tutorials to get you started.

Web Browsing

Web browsing on the Kindle Fire HD is much the same as it is on any other tablet. Amazon has developed a proprietary browser named Silk, claiming a 40% speed bump over other tablet web browsers like Apple's Safari and Google's Chrome. While we're a little skeptical of that claim, it's still a fine browser with some innovative features.

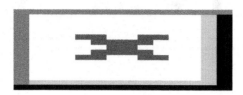

Navigating around the web with Amazon's Silk browser is a snap. Simply tap Web on the home screen, and you'll be taken to the browser. If you've used it before, previews of all of your recently visited websites will show up below the search and address bar. If you need to search for something, just tap inside the search/address bar and type what you're looking for. To go to a specific url (i.e. **www.cnn.com**) simply type in the address and hit enter. That's all there is to it. Navigate your way around the web page using up and down swipes and left to right swipes. To zoom in on a specific section, tap the area with your finger.

If you need to open another web page without closing the one you're currently on, just tap the + symbol in the upper right hand corner. To browse in full screen mode, just tap the full screen button on the bottom of the screen.

To add the webpage you're viewing to your bookmarks, tap the bookmark icon to the left of the navigation bar:

Email, Contacts, Calendar

It seems like everyone nowadays has about thirty "connected" devices capable of delivering your email, keeping track of your contacts and organizing your calendar. The Kindle Fire HD is no exception. In fact, unlike some other tablet devices, the Fire has a pretty great email program. To get started, just tap the Apps menu from the home screen and find the email app. Tap it and fill out the information. If you're using Gmail, Yahoo, or an Enterprise server, you'll also be able to import your contacts and synchronize your calendars. There's nothing for you to do after entering in your login details, it just works.

Reading and sending email is about as intuitive as it gets. After logging in, just open the email app and you'll be greeted with your most recent emails. Just tap to read them, and tap 'respond' on the top of your screen to reply. Tap 'new' to create a new email. Note that the + symbol on the right will bring up a list of contacts that you just imported.

The calendar is just as simple. Just tap the calendar icon on your apps list to open it. Any calendars you've just synced by adding your Yahoo, Gmail, or Enterprise server information will automatically appear. You can add or edit items by tapping on the date of your entry and then tapping the + symbol. The interface is extraordinarily simple, but that's its main strength. Even people who don't use calendar applications could find this useful:

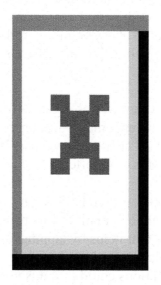

Skype, Facebook and Twitter

For the first time ever, Amazon has added a camera to one of their devices. While it's by no means a professional grade setup, the front-facing camera included with your Kindle Fire HD is more than adequate for making video calls to friends and loved ones. Amazon has partnered with Skype to make it as painless as possible for you to get started.

The Skype application is included with the Kindle Fire HD, so there isn't anything to download. Just head to your apps menu and find it; it's a little blue bubble-looking thing with a white 'S' on it. Tap it to open. If you've already used Skype on your computer or another device, just login; Skype for Kindle Fire HD functions in the exact same way. If you haven't, just tap the little button that says create account and fill out the information it asks you for.

Important note: Assuming you're in America, our country code is +1. Nobody ever tells you that, and Skype won't let you register without adding that to the beginning of your phone number.

Once you're finished setting it up, you're going to need to add some contacts to Skype with. Tap the 'Contacts' button and then the three little squares in the upper-right corner of your device. Tap 'add contacts' and search for your friends and relatives by email address, phone number, or first and last name. Once you've found them, Skype will initiate a request to add you as a friend. Once they approve, you're all set. Simply tap the button that looks like a video camera and that will start a video call with whoever you like, provided they also have a camera on their device. If not, they may see you without you seeing them. You can also make audio-only calls, or even exchange instant messages with your friends, all free of charge. Skype charges a small fee for true text messaging and international calling, but you won't have to worry about that on the Kindle Fire HD.

Facebook has a dedicated app for the Kindle Fire HD as well, though you'll have to download that one from the Amazon App Store. It looks and acts just like Facebook on any other device, though, so you should have no trouble finding your way around. The really cool thing about Facebook and the Kindle Fire HD is the integration.

There are dozens of ways to share the content from your Kindle Fire HD to your Facebook account. Almost anywhere the little share icon shows up, sharing to Facebook is an option. Probably the neatest bit of integration, though, is within your Kindle books: highlight any passage in any book and you can share it to your Facebook Wall. Just tap the share button to bring up the social network dialog box:

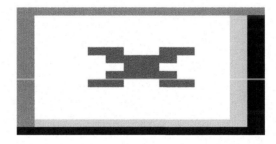

Notice that Twitter is also included by default in your sharing options, provided you linked your Twitter during the Kindle Fire HD's setup process earlier.

Part 3: Advanced Tips and Tricks (and Must-Have Apps)

If you've gotten this far, congratulations! You're officially a Kindle Fire HD power-user. Now that you know what you're doing, we've got a few more things to tell you about. We're going to cram as much information into this section as we can, so we're dispensing with the pictures from here on out.

Ready? Good!

To start, let's take a look at some of the advanced settings on your device.

Settings

Pulling down the notification menu gives you a few options: Volume, Brightness, Orientation Lock, a Syncing toggle, and a shortcut to Wireless settings. Tapping the Wireless icon will bring up a detailed menu, including a toggle for airplane mode and a sub menu for Bluetooth connections.

> *Airplane mode temporarily shuts off your wireless radio, overriding any connection you've made, which is often demanded of you by cranky flight attendants.*

Bluetooth actually works really well on the Kindle Fire HD. With no effort at all, we were able to pair it with an iPhone 4S, a Galaxy S III, and even our car stereo. There were really no settings to fiddle with, we just turned on Bluetooth discovery and were able to send files back and forth with ease.

All the way to the right of the notifications menu, you'll find the word "more" underneath yet another + icon. Tap it to explore the advanced settings menu. From here, you can control every aspect of your Kindle Fire HD that is changeable.

Help & Feedback – If you've got this guide handy, you don't really need to deal with the help portion of this menu, but the "Customer Service" area can be helpful. Tapping it will allow you to send an email to the Amazon support team. Interestingly, you can also elect to have an Amazon support person call your phone right from this menu. We had no reason to use it, but we went through the steps anyway and were promptly phoned by a nice woman who wasn't even remotely upset that we just wanted to say hello.

My Account – This section covers all the accounts and settings that make your Kindle Fire HD *yours*. From here you can de-register your device, add or remove your social networks, and manage the email/contact/calendar accounts you've set up. It's also the only place on the device that will tell you what your @kindle.com email address is. Documents emailed to this address will show up in the Documents menu on your home screen.

Applications – This menu contains all the advanced settings you might need for your applications. Is the constant ding of you email notifications bugging you? You can shut that off here. Want to delete a bunch of apps at once? This is the spot. The most important *hidden* setting of all also resides here: the Silk submenu. Have you noticed that Microsoft's Bing is the default search engine on your device? Kind of weird, isn't it? You can change that to Google or Yahoo from here. You can set the browser to block pop-up ads, and choose whether or not to display websites you visit on the home screen carousel. You can even choose which version of any given website you want to look at, the small-screen optimized mobile page, or the content-rich desktop version. Not every site has both, but it's still nice to be able to choose.

Parental Controls – This menu is a godsend for anyone who lets a child anywhere near the Kindle Fire HD. As we've discussed, it's remarkably easy to empty your bank account filling this device with content. Imagine that you're a little rug rat with no financial accountability! Thankfully, Amazon makes it easy to restrict any aspect of the device. You can lock out purchases, video playback, music listening, book reading, apps, you name it. You can even block access to Wi-Fi. All you have to do is turn on parental controls and choose a password. Now, every activity you've locked down won't function without that password.

> *Amazon has announced an even more comprehensive parental control system for the Kindle Fire HD dubbed "Free Time", but it hasn't yet released it. It's purportedly able to restrict activities to certain amounts of time per day, say 30 minutes of app usage, an hour of web browsing, and 4 hours of book reading. It will also reportedly include up to five "user profiles" to help keep everyone happy. We can't wait to try it out and report back to you.*

Sounds and Display – This menu contains a few of the toggles from the notification dropdown, but it also allows you to mute *all* of those pesky notification sounds, if you so choose. You can also change the sound that notifications make to something that better suits your ears. One very important setting that you'll probably want to change is the screen timeout. This is the amount of time the device will let you not interact with it before shutting the screen off and saving you a little battery life. By default, it's set at 5 minutes, but you can lower it as low as 30 seconds if you want to. Watching videos and reading books will override this setting, so you don't have to worry about that.

Wireless – This is the very same menu we discussed above. You can choose your Wi-Fi network, toggle Airplane Mode, and set up Bluetooth from here.

> *It's also fun to look through the available Wi-Fi networks in your neighborhood. One of my neighbors named their Wi-Fi network "My Wife Snores." It makes me smile every time I see it.*

Device – This is an important menu for a couple of reasons. First, it's where you check to see if Amazon has released any system updates. You'll also be able to find out how much storage and battery life you have left. If you change time zones, you can fix the clock here, and if you run into trouble, you can hit the "reset to factory defaults" button, which will start you over from scratch. The single most important setting here, though, is the "allow installation of applications from unknown sources" toggle. The Amazon App Store doesn't always have every available and compatible app, so you might occasionally need to step outside of their ecosystem. Case in point: we use the cloud file hosting service Dropbox for a lot of things (more on that in our Must-Have Apps section), but the Amazon App Store hasn't made it available yet. After turning this toggle on, we just navigated to **www.dropbox.com** and downloaded the Dropbox app from there. It works perfectly.

> *Although it isn't very common, allowing your device to install unknown apps from the Internet can sometimes have negative consequences. Always make sure that you download and install apps from sources you trust to avoid viruses, key loggers, or any other type of malware.*

Location-based Services – While your device isn't equipped with GPS, Amazon can still figure out where you are by using your Wi-Fi signal. Some apps, like Facebook, use this information to tell other people where you are. Other apps, like Moviefone or Yelp, use it to help you figure out what's around you. Keeping this setting off will keep anyone from knowing where you are at any time. It's important for international spies and anyone else who guards their privacy intensely.

Keyboard – This menu controls, appropriately enough, the keyboard. You can set it to make a distinctive 'click' with each letter press, you can also turn on (or off) automatic capitalization and spell checking. You've probably noticed by now that your device will auto-correct your words as you type. If this annoys you, you can shut it off here.

Security- This menu will allow you to set a lock screen password, keeping everyone but you out of your Kindle Fire HD. The password you choose has nothing to do with parental lock you may have chosen earlier, so be sure to pick something you'll remember. This area also contains settings for corporate deployment of the tablet. These VPN settings and credential verifications will probably never be of use to you, and if they are, the settings will be managed by an IT department, not you.

Legal & Compliance – The last item in the advanced menu is also the least important. This area just houses the terms and conditions and legal notices that nobody ever reads. Amazon includes this section only because they legally have to. The area can be quite useful under the right circumstances, however: if you're having trouble falling asleep, reading a page or two of the safety guidelines will have you snoring in a minute or two, guaranteed.

Sideloading Apps

While the Kindle Fire HD is technically an Android device, we've already mentioned that Amazon won't give you access to the Google Play Store. Instead, they offer a more limited selection through their own store. While this can be helpful, giving Amazon a chance to check on every application to make sure it functions well on the Kindle Fire HD, it can also be frustrating for advanced users. Some apps are just unavailable for no discernible reason. We mentioned Dropbox, but there are literally dozens of other apps that you might want to install. Thankfully, it's super-easy to do.

Sideloading is basically a fancy word for copying apps to your device from your computer. Most free apps can be found by googling the app name with ".apk" appended to it. That's the standard Android application extension, which the Kindle Fire HD uses. Others can be found by going straight to the app developer's website. In either case, you can simply drag and drop the files from your computer into the 'download' folder on your Kindle Fire HD.

> *Not all sideloaded apps will work on your Kindle Fire HD, but a good rule of thumb is: if it works on other 7-inch Android tablets, it'll probably be fine. Devices like the Nexus 7 and the Galaxy Tab 2 are markedly similar inside. You won't do any harm to your Kindle by trying, in any case.*

Appendix: The Best Downloads For Your New Kindle

Games Apps

While the Kindle Fire HD is geared toward book reading and movie watching, the hardware underneath supports a surprising number of intense and satisfying games. Here's our Top Ten list:

10. *Minecraft: Pocket Edition ($6.99)*

If you're at all familiar with this oddly addictive building game, you've probably already downloaded it. For the uninitiated, though, you're in for a real treat. It's one part geometry puzzle, one part Sim City, and two parts Walking Dead. While not quite as robust as its PC or Xbox brethren, the mobile version of this blocky wonderland will definitely keep you building.

9. *Hanging With Friends (Free)*

Zynga has been putting out some amazing social games for Facebook for years. Recently, they've ported that success over to mobile devices. Hanging With Friends is hangman on steroids, played with your friends in the same turn-based way that made Words With Friends so insanely popular last year. You can even chat in-game, giving you a reason to *never* stop playing it.

8. *Jeopardy! HD ($1.99)*

If you've ever felt like you're *too* smart and need to be knocked down a peg or two, this is the game for you. With questions crafted by the same people who create the Jeopardy! Television show, there are a whole bunch of head scratcher-type questions in this game. You can play it in single-player mode, but the real fun starts when you pass it around the room for multiplayer action.

7. *N.O.V.A. 3 ($6.99)*

Easily the most impressive sci-fi game yet released for Kindle Fire HD, N.O.V.A. 3 is part of a longstanding series of first-person-shooters. In this version, you'll be fighting for the safety of the galaxy, from Earth through Volterite City. The graphics are impressive, even by the standards set by our HDTV's with the latest gaming consoles.

6. *Battlefield: Bad Company 2 ($4.99)*

No list of must-have apps would be complete without an epic war game. While not exactly Call of Duty, Battlefield has a lot of fans in the war action genre, and after playing this game on your Kindle Fire HD for awhile, you just might become one of them. It's not just a slimmed down port of the console title, either, its 14 missions are an enhancement to the storyline of its big brother.

5. Madden 12 ($4.99)

Madden football games have been a staple of every video game system since the Sega Genesis, but the last few years have been lightyears ahead of previous generations. Playing Madden on the Kindle Fire HD's gorgeous touchscreen display is one of the most immersive experiences you can have without signing yourself up for training camp.

4. Where's My Water? ($0.99)

This one made its way to the list by accident: leaving the Kindle Fire HD unattended with a young child, even for a moment, will probably result in the acquisition of this addictive Disney physics puzzle game by said child. You'll be pleasantly surprised, however, by the endearing storyline, the complicated puzzles, and the sheer amount of time it takes to beat it. You might even end up calling in sick to work. Don't say we didn't warn you.

3. Cut The Rope HD ($1.99)

If feeding candy to an insatiable monster named Om Nom by cutting ropes with your fingers doesn't sound like a good time to you, you need to check your pulse; you may not be alive anymore. Over 50 million people have downloaded this game so far, and all those people couldn't be wrong, could they?

2. Angry Birds HD ($2.99)

The title that started the casual phone gaming revolution is just as fun and addictive as it was when it was first released. Optimized for the large, high definition 7 inch screen on the Kindle Fire HD, you'll be smashing pigs and reclaiming your eggs in style. We have no idea why this game never gets old, but it's still just about the most fun we've had on the device so far. With one exception…

1. Asphalt 7: Heat ($0.99)

Asphalt 7 is the racing game to end all racing games. With the hyper-realistic physics and ridiculously gorgeous graphics, the fact that you can get behind the wheel of a bunch of amazing cars (Lamborghinis, Ferraris, even the DeLorean!) is just icing on the cake. This game really pushes the limits of what the Kindle Fire HD can do, and it's ridiculously fun too.

Apps

Not everything in life is a game. Sometimes, you need a little productivity. Other times, you need some music and movies. What follows is our Top Ten list of must-have apps (that aren't games). A lot of these apps are completely free. However; some of them require a subscription to the underlying service. Trust us, though, they're all worth it.

10. *Spotify (Free, subscription required)*

Since launching in America last year, Spotify has taken over the music world with its all you can eat business model. It's simple: pay them ten bucks a month and stream literally *all* the music you can dream of, whenever you want to. No limits, no ads, all awesome. They'll give you a free trial, so why not give it a shot?

9. *HBO GO (Free, subscription required)*

HBO, the best premium cable channel of all time, makes this app available to its subscribers free of charge. It includes just about every original show they've ever aired (including The Sopranos, Six Feet Under, The Wire, Sex and The City, etc.) and a whole lot of movies, documentaries and sports programs. Did we mention it's completely free?

8. *Hulu Plus (Free, subscription required)*

Hulu has been around for awhile as a Netflix competitor, but their focus on just-aired TV content puts them slightly ahead for some people. Just like Spotify, they'll give you a free trial, but after that, it'll cost you $7.99 a month to keep up on Gossip Girl. Worth it? You decide.

7. *Dropbox (Free)*

We discussed our enthusiasm for Dropbox earlier in this book, while lamenting the fact that it's not officially available in the Amazon App Store. Point your browser to their website to download it anyway, and get five gigs of on-demand storage for absolutely no money. You can even set it to automatically upload any picture you take with your Kindle Fire HD. For that alone, this is a must-have.

6. *BeyondPod Podcast Manager ($6.99)*

Podcasts are an often overlooked part of Internet culture. Think of them as weekly radio shows for the digital age. This is the best Podcast manager on the market, even better than iTunes, who invented the concept. You can browse a *huge* selection of content, everything from NPR's *This American Life* and Discovery's *Stuff You Should Know* all the way through Kevin Smith's *Smodcast* and *Hollywood Babble-on*, this app is essential for anyone who loves learning (and laughing.)

5. Instapaper ($2.99)

The concept is simple: take all the stuff you want to read on the web, cut out the pictures and the ads and all the other junk, and make it available for offline viewing. This app is *perfect* for long train rides, plane trips, or anywhere where access to the Internet isn't a possibility.

4. Comics (Free, w/ in-app purchases)

The Kindle Fire HD has a gorgeous screen, so why not meld it with your favorite comic books? There are a few different comic book apps in the store, but this is the most comprehensive by far: you can get everything from Marvel superheroes to The Walking Dead right from the app and begin reading in seconds. It's also the only app to incorporate a "guided view", which will pan the screen and zoom in on the important parts as you read them.

3. Wikipedia (Free)

You know it, you love it: Wikipedia is the encyclopedia for the digital age. It's an indispensible app that'll let you look up everything from how the Electoral College works to Monica Lewinsky's birthday. The fact that they give away such an invaluable resource is astounding.

2. Wolfram Alpha ($3.99)

Wolfram Alpha is sort of the Wikipedia for science geeks. Enter equations, technical questions, or even periodic elements and the Wolfram Alpha engine will give you all sorts of collated data to explore. Despite its incredible sophistication, it also makes a handy tip calculator.

1. Office Suite Professional Pro 6 ($14.99)

The Cadillac of mobile office suites, Professional Pro 6 packs a real punch. You can do just about anything with this app: word processing, spreadsheets, presentations, PDF conversions, you name it. You might be a little wary of the price tag, but this app is really about a dozen apps wrapped into one.

So there you have it. Amazon's Kindle Fire HD is a sleek and powerful tablet that's sure to give you a lot of enjoyment. Now that you've got the tools to unlock the device's true power, there's no limit to what you can do with it. We hope you've found this guide fun and informative. Be sure to check out our other guides at http://www.minutehelpguides.com/.

About Minute Help Press

Minute Help Press is building a library of books for people with only minutes to spare. Follow @minutehelp on Twitter to receive the latest information about free and paid publications from Minute Help Press, or visit minutehelp.com.

CPSIA information can be obtained
at www.ICGtesting.com
Printed in the USA
LVOW03s2118190117

521542LV00003B/192/P